PROUDLY DESIGNED ON THE UPPER WEST SIDE
(OF KANSAS CITY).

A BILLION* RANDOM ACTS OF KINDNESS THAT WILL EVEN CHEER UP A JERK.

A PROMPTED JOURNAL

DISCLAIMER

X X X

LOOK, DON'T TAKE THIS TOO SERIOUS.

WE MADE THIS JOURNAL TO SPREAD A
LITTLE BIT OF JOY, BECAUSE, WELL, THE
WORLD CAN BE KIND OF A DOWNER
SOMETIMES.

SO WE FILLED IT WITH A TON OF KIND
(& HOPEFULLY FUN) WAYS TO BRIGHTEN
SOMEONE'S DAY A BIT. USE THEM AS
INSPIRATION, BUT A PREREQUISITE HERE
IS COMMON SENSE (AND A SENSE OF
HUMOR). DON'T DO ANYTHING ILLEGAL,
OR ANYTHING THAT WOULD EMBARRASS
OR HURT OTHERS...AND WE'RE NOT
RESPONSIBLE IF YOU DO.

ANYWAY, HAVE FUN...AND KEEP GOING
WHERE WE LEFT OFF. IN FACT, WE GAVE
YOU SOME SPACE TO ADD YOUR OWN IN
THE BACK OF THE BOOK. WE'D LOVE
TO SEE WHAT YOU COME UP WITH.
YOU CAN CONSIDER IT JUST ONE MORE
ACT OF KINDNESS.

@ BRASSMONKEYGOODS

THIS JOURNAL IS DEDICATED
TO ALL OF THE PEOPLE THAT HAVE
GONE OUT OF THEIR WAY TO BE
UNNECESSARILY KIND TO US OVER
THE YEARS. WE WERE LIKELY TOO
SOCIALLY AWKWARD TO SAY THANKS.

X X X

SO, UH, THANKS.

HOW TO USE THIS JOURNAL

A TUTORIAL

THE GOAL OF THIS BOOK IS TO SPREAD A LITTLE KINDNESS INTO THE WORLD. THAT'S IT, AND NOTHING MORE. WE HAVE NO AGENDA. NO BROADER MESSAGE TO SELL. WE JUST WANT PEOPLE TO SMILE AND ENJOY BEING ALIVE...NO MATTER HOW STUPID LIFE CAN BE SOMETIMES.

SPOILER ALERT: REALLY STUPID.

THAT SAID, WHY DOES BEING KIND HAVE TO BE SO FREAKING BOOORING? PEOPLE JUST GO AROUND WEARING 'BE KIND TO EACH OTHER' T-SHIRTS AND PRETTY MUCH LEAVE IT AT THAT. IT'S LIKE WE ONLY HAVE TO GENTLY WHISPER 'YOU ARE ENOUGH' INTO STRANGERS EARS TO MAGICALLY MAKE THEM FEEL APPRECIATED. WE THINK WE CAN ALL DO BETTER THAN THAT.

THAT'S WHERE THIS JOURNAL COMES IN.

WE'VE DONE OUR BEST TO PACK IT FULL OF KIND (AND FUN) THINGS TO DO FOR YOUR FRIENDS, FAMILY, AND...HONESTLY...COMPLETE STRANGERS. SIMPLY GO THROUGH THE BOOK AND DO AS MANY AS YOU CAN. WE'VE EVEN INCLUDED SPACE TO REFLECT ON THE REACTIONS YOU GET...AND MAYBE EVEN *GASP* HOW DOING THESE THINGS MADE YOU FEEL. EW, RIGHT?

SOME ARE SWEET, SOME ARE WEIRD, SOME MIGHT EVEN BE KIND OF HARD TO PULL OFF. BUT TRY. AS YOU DO THEM THOUGH, PLEASE SHARE PICTURES AND STORIES WITH YOUR FRIENDS (AND US @BRASSMONKEYGOODS). WE'D LOVE TO DO OUR PART TO HELP THE INTERNET FEEL A LITTLE LESS LIKE THE WORLD IS ENDING AND EVERYTHING IS TERRIBLE.

GO ON A REVERSE PICK-POCKETING
SPREE BY SNEAKING FIVE DOLLAR BILLS
INTO STRANGERS' POCKETS.

WHAT WAS THE RESPONSE?

TAKE A PICTURE OF A THANK YOU CARD
AND TEXT IT TO YOUR PARENTS. INCLUDE THE
NOTE 'MONEY DOESN'T GROW ON TREES.'

WHAT WAS THE RESPONSE?

PICK UP ALL THE TRASH ON A STREET IN YOUR NEIGHBORHOOD. WEAR AN ORANGE JUMPSUIT TO CONFUSE THE NEIGHBORS.

WHAT WAS THE RESPONSE?

ILLUSTRATE THE EXPERIENCE

SURPRISE ALL OF YOUR EMPLOYEES WITH A
SPONTANEOUS PAID DAY OFF. NO EMPLOYEES?
BUY A COPY OF THIS BOOK FOR YOUR BOSS.

WHAT WAS THE RESPONSE?

TAKE FIFTY DOLLARS IN QUARTERS TO A
PETTING ZOO AND PAY FOR EVERY KID UNTIL
YOU RUN OUT (OR THE GOATS VOMIT).

WHAT WAS THE RESPONSE?

WRITE AN ONLINE REVIEW FOR
YOUR FAVORITE RESTAURANT, BUT DO IT
IN THIRD PERSON.

WHAT WAS THE RESPONSE?

VISIT YOUR OLDEST LIVING RELATIVE
AND SPEND THE ENTIRE DAY WITH THEM.
ASK THEM TO TELL YOU STORIES.

WHAT WAS THE RESPONSE?

YELL G-RATED COMPLIMENTS AT NEARBY
CONSTRUCTION WORKERS, LIKE 'OH YEAH, I
BET YOU GIVE REALLY GOOD HUGS BABY!'

WHAT WAS THE RESPONSE?

DRAW A PORTRAIT OF ONE OF YOUR FRIENDS AND GIVE IT TO THEM. NOW GUILT THEM INTO HANGING IT UP.

DON'T HAVE A CANVAS HANDY? USE THIS:

SIGN YOUR MASTERPIECE

MAKE A LIST OF ALL THE THINGS THAT
YOU LIKE ABOUT YOUR SERVER, AND LEAVE
IT IN THE BILL (WITH A GIANT TIP).

WAIT UNTIL YOUR NEIGHBORS AREN'T HOME AND MOW THEIR LAWN. KEEP DOING IT EVERY WEEK UNTIL THEY FIGURE IT OUT.

. . . .

. . . .

. . . .

. . . .

. . . .

. . . .

———————— WHAT WAS THE RESPONSE? ————————

BUY A BOUQUET AT THE LOCAL FLOWER SHOP, AND GIVE IT TO THE PERSON THAT RANG YOU UP.

. . . .

. . . .

. . . .

. . . .

. . . .

. . . .

———————— WHAT WAS THE RESPONSE? ————————

RANDOM ACTS OF KINDNESS • NO. 13

SURPRISE A CHILD THAT YOU DON'T LIVE WITH (AND RARELY VISIT) WITH A SLIDE WHISTLE RIGHT BEFORE YOU LEAVE.

. . . .
. . . .

WHAT WAS THE RESPONSE?

RANDOM ACTS OF KINDNESS • NO. 14

WHILE YOU'RE AT A GAS STATION, SECRETLY WASH PEOPLE'S WINDSHIELDS WHEN THEY GO INSIDE TO PAY.

. . . .
. . . .

WHAT WAS THE RESPONSE?

RANDOM ACTS OF KINDNESS • NO. 15

AFTER A RAINSTORM, OFFER TO GIVE PEOPLE PIGGY BACK RIDES OVER ANY LARGE PUDDLES IN THE STREET.

. . . .
. . . .

WHAT WAS THE RESPONSE?

BAKE SOME HOMEMADE BROWNIES FOR ALL OF YOUR COWORKERS AT THE OFFICE—MARIJUANA OPTIONAL.

. . . .

. . . .

. . . .

. . . .

. . . .

. . . .

. . . .

. . . .

. . . .

. . . .

——————— WHAT WAS THE RESPONSE? ———————

FIGURE 1

THE NEXT TIME YOU GO TO THE DMV, DRAW A PICTURE OF THE PERSON WORKING THE COUNTER AND GIVE IT TO THEM.

DON'T HAVE A CANVAS HANDY? USE THIS:

SIGN YOUR MASTERPIECE

ON YOUR NEXT FLIGHT, BRING FULL SIZE
CHOCOLATE BARS FOR EVERYONE IN COACH.
GIVE FIRST-CLASS THE 'FUN SIZE.'

WHAT WAS THE RESPONSE?

COOK A FOUR-COURSE MEAL FOR YOUR
PARENTS. LOCK THE DOOR & DON'T LET THEM
LEAVE UNTIL THEY HAVE HAPPY PLATES.

WHAT WAS THE RESPONSE?

FLAG DOWN THE ICE CREAM TRUCK AND BUY A POPSICLE FOR EVERYONE IN THE VICINITY (INCLUDING THE DRIVER).

WHAT WAS THE RESPONSE?

FIGURE 1

SERENADE THE CASHIER AT YOUR LOCAL
SUPERMARKET. BRING A GUITAR. BONUS POINTS
IF YOU DON'T KNOW HOW TO PLAY IT.

. . . .
. . . .

——— WHAT WAS THE RESPONSE? ———

WHEN A FRIEND ASKS FOR A RIDE TO
THE AIRPORT, OFFER TO DRIVE THEM ALL THE
WAY TO THEIR DESTINATION INSTEAD.

. . . .
. . . .

——— WHAT WAS THE RESPONSE? ———

VOLUNTEER AT A LOCAL SOUP
KITCHEN, BUT INSIST THAT YOU GET TO
HOLD THE LADLE.

. . . .
. . . .

——— WHAT WAS THE RESPONSE? ———

RANDOM ACTS OF KINDNESS • NO. 24

TREAT THE CUSTODIAL STAFF AT YOUR
OFFICE TO DRINKS AFTER THEY GET OFF
WORK (ALSO, FIND A BAR OPEN AT 6 AM).

WHAT WAS THE RESPONSE?

RANDOM ACTS OF KINDNESS • NO. 25

HOLD THE DOOR OPEN AT A RETIREMENT
HOME FOR OVER AN HOUR (DESPITE THEIR
REPEATED REQUESTS TO STOP).

WHAT WAS THE RESPONSE?

BUY A COFFEE FOR THE SADDEST-LOOKING PERSON AT THE COFFEE SHOP.

——————— WHAT WAS THE RESPONSE? ———————

OFFER YOUR SEAT TO LITERALLY EVERY SINGLE PERSON THAT GETS ON THE BUS AFTER YOU (NO MATTER HOW EMPTY IT IS).

——————— WHAT WAS THE RESPONSE? ———————

HELP STRANGERS CARRY THEIR GROCERIES. ALSO, ASSURE SAID STRANGERS THAT YOU AREN'T STEALING THEIR GROCERIES.

. . . .

. . . .

. . . .

. . . .

. . . .

. . . .

. . . .

. . . .

. . . .

. . . .

——————— WHAT WAS THE RESPONSE? ———————

FIGURE 1

**WRITE A POEM ABOUT YOUR FAVORITE
FAST FOOD CHAIN, AND SEND IT TO THEM.
(BONUS POINTS IF IT'S A LIMERICK).**

ENCOURAGE A FRIEND TO PURSUE THEIR
DREAMS. UNLESS THEY DREAM OF MURDER, IN
WHICH CASE, ENCOURAGE THEM NOT TO.

WHAT WAS THE RESPONSE?

BUY A CD FROM A STREET MUSICIAN,
EVEN THOUGH YOU HAVE ABSOLUTELY NO
WAY TO ACTUALLY PLAY A CD.

WHAT WAS THE RESPONSE?

GIVE A KISS TO A STRANGER – BUT
A HERSHEY'S KISS, SO IT'S NOT SEXUAL
HARASSMENT.

WHAT WAS THE RESPONSE?

STAND ON THE SIDEWALK AND CLAP FOR PEOPLE AFTER THEY SUCCESSFULLY PARALLEL PARK.

WHAT WAS THE RESPONSE?

FIGURE 1

START A NETFLIX ACCOUNT JUST TO SHARE W/ OTHERS...BUT WATCH WEIRD STUFF ON IT 1ST TO THROW OFF THE RECOMMENDATIONS.

. . . .
. . . .
. . . .
. . . .
. . . .
. . . .
. . . .
. . . .
. . . .
. . . .

—————— WHAT WAS THE RESPONSE? ——————

FIGURE 1

SHOVEL YOUR NEIGHBORS DRIVEWAY
THE NEXT TIME IT SNOWS, AND USE IT TO
MAKE A SNOWMAN IN THEIR LIKENESS.

WHAT WAS THE RESPONSE?

BUY OUT A LOCAL KID'S LEMONADE
STAND. NOW HELP THEM FRANCHISE...AFTER
YOU DRINK ALL OF SAID LEMONADE.

WHAT WAS THE RESPONSE?

DO THE DISHES.
EVEN WHEN IT'S NOT YOUR TURN.
AT AN OLIVE GARDEN.

· ·

· ·

· ·

· ·

· ·

· ·

——————— WHAT WAS THE RESPONSE? ———————

STAND IN A REALLY LONG LINE, AND
WHEN IT'S ALMOST YOUR TURN, SWITCH
SPOTS WITH THE VERY LAST PERSON.

· ·

· ·

· ·

· ·

· ·

· ·

——————— WHAT WAS THE RESPONSE? ———————

SELECT A RANDOM PERSON'S WEDDING REGISTRY ONLINE AND BUY ONE OF THEIR ITEMS. INCLUDE A CRYPTIC GIFT TAG.

DRAW A PICTURE OF WHAT YOU BOUGHT THEM:

SIGN YOUR MASTERPIECE

LEAVE AN ANONYMOUS NOTE ON THE WINDSHIELD OF A RANDOM PARKED CAR. TELL THEM THEY'RE BEAUTIFUL.

RANDOM ACTS OF KINDNESS • NO. 41

FIND THE BEST PHOTO OF A FRIEND ON
YOUR PHONE AND HAVE IT FRAMED FOR
THEM. FRAME THE WORST ONE, TOO.

WHAT WAS THE RESPONSE?

RANDOM ACTS OF KINDNESS • NO. 42

TAKE ALL OF YOUR OLD VIDEO GAMES AND
DONATE THEM TO A CHILDREN'S HOSPITAL.
SERIOUSLY, YOU'RE OLD. IT'S TIME.

WHAT WAS THE RESPONSE?

RANDOM ACTS OF KINDNESS • NO. 43

TRY TO GO AN ENTIRE DAY WITHOUT SAYING
ANYTHING NEGATIVE. YOU'LL FAIL, BUT AT
LEAST YOU TRIED.

WHAT WAS THE RESPONSE?

**BUY CHEAP UMBRELLAS IN BULK, THEN
STAND ON A STREET CORNER AND HAND THEM
OUT TO WET PEOPLE ON A RAINY DAY.**

WHAT WAS THE RESPONSE?

**GIVE A LONG BACK MASSAGE TO A LOVED
ONE. LIKE, JUST KEEP GOING UNTIL IT GETS
A LITTLE AWKWARD.**

WHAT WAS THE RESPONSE?

GET A WAD OF SINGLES FROM THE BANK AND HIDE THEM IN BOOKS AT YOUR LOCAL LIBRARY.

. . . .
. . . .
. . . .
. . . .
. . . .
. . . .
. . . .
. . . .
. . . .
. . . .

———————— WHAT WAS THE RESPONSE? ————————

FIGURE 1

GIVE EVERYONE AT YOUR LOCAL RETIREMENT HOME A HUG — RIGHT AFTER 4 NEGATIVE PCR TESTS AND A VACCINATION.

————— WHAT WAS THE RESPONSE? —————

FIGURE 1

OFFER TO HELP A FRIEND MOVE. CONSIDER IT A BONUS IF THEY PLAN ON MOVING.

WHAT WAS THE RESPONSE?

DONATE TO A GOFUNDME FOR A STRANGER GOING THROUGH CANCER. SORRY FOR THE DOWNER.

WHAT WAS THE RESPONSE?

LEAVE A ROLL OF QUARTERS ON A WASHING MACHINE AT THE NEAREST LAUNDROMAT.

———————— WHAT WAS THE RESPONSE? ————————

FIGURE 1

PICK UP ALL THE DOG POOP AT YOUR
LOCAL PARK, BUT LIKE, WITH BAGS, NOT
YOUR HANDS.

. . . .

. . . .

. . . .

. . . .

. . . .

. . . .

WHAT WAS THE RESPONSE?

GO SEE A LOCAL BAND PERFORM & ASK
FOR THEIR AUTOGRAPHS AFTERWARDS,
REGARDLESS OF HOW TERRIBLE THEY WERE.

. . . .

. . . .

. . . .

. . . .

. . . .

. . . .

WHAT WAS THE RESPONSE?

MAKE A CLOTHING ITEM FOR A
FRIEND. EVEN BETTER IF YOU HAVE NO
IDEA HOW TO SEW.

WHAT WAS THE RESPONSE?

TRACK DOWN THE ADDRESS OF A FAVORITE
TEACHER AND SEND THEM A LITER OF APPLE
BRANDY AND AN APOLOGY.

WHAT WAS THE RESPONSE?

PAINT A PICTURE OF SOMEONE'S HOUSE AND LEAVE IT IN THEIR MAILBOX.

DON'T HAVE A CANVAS HANDY? USE THIS:

SIGN YOUR MASTERPIECE

BECOME A PEN PAL WITH A PRISONER. PRO-TIP: USE A PO BOX — YOU KNOW, JUST IN CASE THEY'RE MURDERY.

RANDOM ACTS OF KINDNESS • NO. 57

BUY A RANDOM MATCHBOX CAR, THEN DRIVE AROUND UNTIL YOU FIND THAT EXACT VEHICLE. LEAVE IT ON THEIR WINDSHIELD.

. . . .
. . . .
. . . .
. . . .
. . . .
. . . .

———— WHAT WAS THE RESPONSE? ————

RANDOM ACTS OF KINDNESS • NO. 58

HELP SOMEONE GET THEIR STROLLER UP A FLIGHT OF STAIRS. YOU SHOULD PROBABLY ASK FIRST THOUGH.

. . . .
. . . .
. . . .
. . . .
. . . .
. . . .

———— WHAT WAS THE RESPONSE? ————

RANDOM ACTS OF KINDNESS • NO. 59

BUY POPCORN FOR THE PERSON IN FRONT OF YOU AT THE MOVIES. UNLESS YOU'RE 7' TALL — THEN GIVE IT TO THE PERSON BEHIND YOU.

. . . .

. . . .

——————— WHAT WAS THE RESPONSE? ———————

RANDOM ACTS OF KINDNESS • NO. 60

THROW A SURPRISE PARTY FOR YOUR BEST FRIEND ON SOME RANDOM DAY & INVITE ALL OF THEIR OTHER FRIENDS.

. . . .

. . . .

——————— WHAT WAS THE RESPONSE? ———————

RANDOM ACTS OF KINDNESS • NO. 61

RESCUE A STRAY DOG AND TAKE IT TO THE LOCAL SHELTER. INSIST THAT THEY NAME IT 'STEVE.'

. . . .

. . . .

——————— WHAT WAS THE RESPONSE? ———————

ANONYMOUSLY ORDER NACHOS FOR EVERY
TABLE AT YOUR LOCAL PUB. GET SOME FOR
YOURSELF, TOO. YOU KNOW, FOR CAMOUFLAGE.

WHAT WAS THE RESPONSE?

FIGURE 1

DRAW A PICTURE OF YOUR FAVORITE
CELEBRITY & SEND IT TO THEM ON TWITTER.
MAKE THEM FEEL BAD UNTIL THEY LIKE IT.

DON'T HAVE A CANVAS HANDY? USE THIS:

SIGN YOUR MASTERPIECE

BAKE A CAKE FOR YOUR MAIL CARRIER &
WRITE 'YOU REALLY DELIVER – EXCEPT ON
SUNDAYS APPARENTLY' ON THE TOP.

WHAT WAS THE RESPONSE?

BUY A GIFT CARD AT YOUR FAVORITE
LOCAL RESTAURANT & GIVE IT TO SOMEONE
WAITING TO BE SEATED AS YOU LEAVE.

WHAT WAS THE RESPONSE?

TELL A STRANGER ON THE INTERNET THAT YOU APPRECIATE THEM. BE CLEAR THAT YOU AREN'T BEING SARCASTIC – REPEATEDLY.

WHAT WAS THE RESPONSE?

FIGURE 1

GO TO AN AMERICAN CITIZENSHIP CEREMONY, AND GIVE A CAN OF SPRAY CHEESE TO EACH PERSON BECOMING A CITIZEN. U.S.A! U.S.A!

WHAT WAS THE RESPONSE?

BECOME A BIG BROTHER OR BIG SISTER. THROUGH THE ORGANIZATION...DON'T FORCE YOUR PARENTS TO HAVE SEX AT THIS AGE.

WHAT WAS THE RESPONSE?

GO TO THE ARCADE AND PAY FOR PEOPLE TO PLAY SKEE-BALL AGAINST YOU IN THE NEXT LANE OVER. WINNER TAKES ALL (TICKETS).

WHAT WAS THE RESPONSE?

HELP AN ANIMAL CROSS THE
ROAD. BONUS POINTS IF IT'S ACTUALLY
A CHICKEN.

. . . .

. . . .

. . . .

. . . .

. . . .

. . . .

WHAT WAS THE RESPONSE?

HIRE A SINGING TELEGRAM TO TELL
YOUR MOM THAT YOU LOVE HER AND TO GET
OFF YOUR BACK ABOUT NOT CALLING MORE.

. . . .

. . . .

. . . .

. . . .

. . . .

. . . .

WHAT WAS THE RESPONSE?

RANDOM ACTS OF KINDNESS • NO. 72

**BUY 10 BOTTLED WATERS IN THE AIRPORT &
GIVE THEM TO PEOPLE WHO GET THEIRS TAKEN
AWAY BY TSA. THIS WILL COST YOU $2,000.**

. . . .
. . . .
. . . .
. . . .
. . . .
. . . .

——— WHAT WAS THE RESPONSE? ———

RANDOM ACTS OF KINDNESS • NO. 73

**CALL IN A PIZZA DELIVERY FOR A RANDOM
HOUSE IN YOUR NEIGHBORHOOD. PRE-PAY
(W/ A TIP) & EXPLAIN THAT IT'S A SURPRISE.**

. . . .
. . . .
. . . .
. . . .
. . . .
. . . .

——— WHAT WAS THE RESPONSE? ———

PUT 2 DOLLARS IN A VENDING MACHINE, BUT DON'T PICK ANYTHING. JUST LEAVE A POST-IT THAT SAYS 'YOU'RE WELCOME.'

. . . .

. . . .

. . . .

. . . .

. . . .

. . . .

. . . .

. . . .

. . . .

. . . .

———————— WHAT WAS THE RESPONSE? ————————

FIGURE 1

MAKE A LIST OF THE AMAZING THINGS YOUR DAD DID FOR YOU GROWING UP. THEN GIVE HIM THE LIST & ASK FOR 20 BUCKS.

. . . .

. . . .

. . . .

. . . .

. . . .

. . . .

. . . .

. . . .

. . . .

. . . .

. . . .

. . . .

. . . .

. . . .

. . . .

. . . .

. . . .

. . . .

. . . .

. . . .

——————— NO PAPER? WELL, YOU'RE IN LUCK. ———————

CHOOSE WHERE YOU & YOUR PARTNER EAT NEXT TIME, INSTEAD OF INEVITABLY SCREAMING 'I DON'T CARE, YOU PICK!' AT EACH OTHER.

WHAT WAS THE RESPONSE?

HOLD A FREE CAR WASH ON YOUR STREET. DON'T ACCEPT TIPS, AND THREATEN TO DANCE INAPPROPRIATELY IF THEY INSIST.

WHAT WAS THE RESPONSE?

BUY A BUNCH OF BALLOONS FOR A CHILD. THEY HAVE TO BLOW THEM UP THOUGH. TELL THEM THAT'S THE FUN PART.

WHAT WAS THE RESPONSE?

OFFER TO BABYSIT FOR A FRIEND THAT COULD
USE A NIGHT OUT. AND THEN IN HINDSIGHT,
NEVER DO THAT AGAIN. HOLY CRAP.

. . . .
. . . .
. . . .
. . . .
. . . .
. . . .
. . . .
. . . .
. . . .
. . . .
. . . .

WHAT WAS THE RESPONSE?

FIGURE 1

GO TO CUSTOMER SERVICE & DEMAND TO SPEAK TO A MANAGER. TELL THEM HOW GREAT THEIR EMPLOYEES ARE WHILE POINTING AGGRESSIVELY.

. . . .

. . . .

. . . .

. . . .

. . . .

. . . .

. . . .

. . . .

. . . .

. . . .

——————— WHAT WAS THE RESPONSE? ———————

FIGURE 1

INVITE YOUR FRIENDS TO A RESTAURANT ON
YOUR BIRTHDAY, BUT AT THE END OF THE NIGHT,
PAY THEIR TABS. SO MAYBE GO TO ARBY'S.

· ·

· ·

· ·

· ·

· ·

· ·

———————— WHAT WAS THE RESPONSE? ————————

DRESS UP LIKE A SUPERHERO & WAVE TO
THE KIDS ON THE SCHOOL BUS — AND ALSO HOPE
THAT IT'S NOT FULL OF HIGH SCHOOLERS.

· ·

· ·

· ·

· ·

· ·

· ·

———————— WHAT WAS THE RESPONSE? ————————

BECOME AN ORGAN DONOR.
AND IF YOU HAVE A SPARE PIANO,
BECOME A PIANO DONOR.

WHAT WAS THE RESPONSE?

OFFER TO WALK YOUR NEIGHBOR'S DOG.
JUST REMEMBER THAT YOU ULTIMATELY
HAVE TO GIVE IT BACK.

WHAT WAS THE RESPONSE?

DRAW THE COVER OF A SLEAZY ROMANCE
NOVEL — BUT WITH YOUR S.O. SHIRTLESS ON
THAT HORSE. NOW PUT IT ON THE FRIDGE.

DON'T HAVE A CANVAS HANDY? USE THIS:

SIGN YOUR MASTERPIECE

MAKE A MIXED TAPE FOR SOMEONE. OR, IN LIEU OF FINDING A WALKMAN, JUST WRITE DOWN A PLAYLIST. THEY HAVE GOOGLE.

BRING SOMEONE BREAKFAST IN BED. THIS
ONE WORKS BETTER IF YOU KNOW THEM & ARE
SUPPOSED TO HAVE ACCESS TO THEIR HOUSE.

. . . .

. . . .

WHAT WAS THE RESPONSE?

COMPLIMENT SOMEONE ON THEIR HAT.
HATS ARE ALWAYS RISKY. COURAGE LIKE THAT
DESERVES TO BE RECOGNIZED.

. . . .

. . . .

WHAT WAS THE RESPONSE?

FILL A GIANT PIÑATA WITH CANDY AND
HANG IT FROM A TREE OVER A PUBLIC
SIDEWALK. HIT IT ONCE AND RUN.

. . . .

. . . .

WHAT WAS THE RESPONSE?

BUY AN EXTRA LARGE PIZZA FOR CARRY-OUT, AND WALK AROUND OFFERING EVERYONE A SLICE UNTIL IT'S GONE.

. . . .

. . . .

. . . .

. . . .

. . . .

. . . .

WHAT WAS THE RESPONSE?

RETURN ALL OF THE LOOSE SHOPPING CARTS IN THE PARKING LOT TO THE CART RETURN. SERIOUSLY, PEOPLE ARE ANIMALS.

. . . .

. . . .

. . . .

. . . .

. . . .

. . . .

WHAT WAS THE RESPONSE?

LEAVE A COOLER FULL OF COLD DRINKS OUT FOR YOUR GARBAGE COLLECTORS—AND MAYBE A SIGN THAT SAYS NOT TO THROW IT AWAY.

. . . .

. . . .

. . . .

. . . .

. . . .

. . . .

. . . .

. . . .

. . . .

. . . .

—————— WHAT WAS THE RESPONSE? ——————

FIGURE 1

HOLD THE DOOR OPEN FOR SOMEONE,
REGARDLESS OF HOW FAR AWAY THEY ARE.
IN FACT, THE FARTHER THE BETTER.

——————————— WHAT WAS THE RESPONSE? ———————————

FIGURE 1

RANDOM ACTS OF KINDNESS • NO. 94

**TELL THE CASHIER YOU CAN'T DECIDE ON A
CANDY BAR, AND ASK WHAT THEIR FAVORITE IS.
BUY IT, AND HAND IT TO THEM AS YOU LEAVE.**

. . . .
. . . .
. . . .
. . . .
. . . .
. . . .

———————— WHAT WAS THE RESPONSE? ————————

RANDOM ACTS OF KINDNESS • NO. 95

**START A BAND & NAME IT AFTER YOUR FRIEND.
APOLOGIZE IN ADVANCE THAT YOU DON'T YET
KNOW HOW TO PLAY AND/OR SING.**

. . . .
. . . .
. . . .
. . . .
. . . .
. . . .

———————— WHAT WAS THE RESPONSE? ————————

RANDOM ACTS OF KINDNESS · NO. 96

MAKE A LIST OF ALL YOUR FAVORITE CANNED FOODS. NOW BUY THEM & DROP THEM OFF AT A FOOD BANK. KEEP ONE CAN, YOU DESERVE IT.

NO PAPER? WELL, YOU'RE IN LUCK.

BUY DONUTS FROM TWO COMPETING BAKERIES
AND GIVE THEM TO EACH OTHER. THROW IN
$10 TOO. THEY'RE PROBABLY SICK OF DONUTS.

. . . .
. . . .

——— WHAT WAS THE RESPONSE? ———

ON YOUR NEXT BEACH VACATION,
FIND A GIANT PALM FROND AND FAN PEOPLE
LAYING BY THE POOL.

. . . .
. . . .

——— WHAT WAS THE RESPONSE? ———

GO WATCH A MARATHON AND GIVE OUT
AS MANY HIGH FIVES TO THE RUNNERS
AS POSSIBLE.

. . . .
. . . .

——— WHAT WAS THE RESPONSE? ———

RANDOM ACTS OF KINDNESS · NO. 100

AFTER A SNOW STORM, FILL A BIG THERMOS
WITH HOT CHOCOLATE & DRIVE AROUND. GIVE
A CUP OF IT TO ANYONE OUT SHOVELING.

WHAT WAS THE RESPONSE?

RANDOM ACTS OF KINDNESS · NO. 101

CONTRIBUTE TO A BLM ORGANIZATION IN
THE NAME OF A RACIST FAMILY MEMBER—SIGN
THEM UP FOR THEIR NEWSLETTER TOO!

WHAT WAS THE RESPONSE?

TELL YOUR PARTNER THAT YOU DREW THEM
A BATH. YOU BETTER ALSO FILL A BATHTUB
WITH WATER, OR THEY'LL MURDER YOU.

DON'T HAVE A CANVAS HANDY? USE THIS:

SIGN YOUR MASTERPIECE

DRAW A SELF PORTRAIT AND SEND IT TO
YOUR PARENTS. NOW GUILT THEM INTO MAKING
IT THE BACKGROUND ON THEIR PHONE.

DON'T HAVE A CANVAS HANDY? USE THIS:

SIGN YOUR MASTERPIECE

USE CHALK TO DRAW A HOPSCOTCH COURT
OUTSIDE A LOCAL BAR. THEY'LL HAVE NO IDEA
HOW TO PLAY, BUT IT'LL BE FUN TO WATCH.

WHAT WAS THE RESPONSE?

PUT A GIFT CARD IN A WRAPPED BOX & LEAVE
IT IN THE BACK SEAT OF AN ESPECIALLY GOOD
TAXI/UBER. WRITE THEIR NAME ON THE TAG.

WHAT WAS THE RESPONSE?

GET A BUNCH OF LOCAL POSTCARDS & USE GOOGLE MAPS TO FIND RANDOM HOUSES ALL OVER THE COUNTRY TO SEND THEM TO.

. . . .

. . . .

———— WHAT WAS THE RESPONSE? ————

SECRETLY BUY ART FROM A FRIEND'S ONLINE SHOP & HAVE IT FRAMED ON YOUR WALL WHEN THEY COME OVER. ADD A LITTLE PLAQUE.

. . . .

. . . .

———— WHAT WAS THE RESPONSE? ————

WHEN THE HOT DOG VENDOR COMES AROUND AT A BASEBALL GAME, GET ONE FOR EVERYONE IN YOUR ROW. ALSO, SIT IN A SHORT ROW.

. . . .

. . . .

———— WHAT WAS THE RESPONSE? ————

GIVE A GUY A COMPLIMENT. ANY COMPLIMENT.
THEIR CLOTHES. THEIR HAIR. THE FACT THAT
THEY EXIST. ANYTHING. WE'RE DESPERATE.

....

....

....

....

....

....

....

....

....

....

WHAT WAS THE RESPONSE?

FIGURE 1

ASK A FRIEND'S KID TO DRAW A PICTURE OF THEIR DAD, AND GET IT PRINTED ONTO A T-SHIRT.

DON'T HAVE A CANVAS HANDY? USE THIS:

SIGN YOUR MASTERPIECE

BUY A GIANT BAG OF GOOGLY EYES ONLINE,
AND SPEND THE REST OF YOUR LIFE PUTTING
THEM ON LITERALLY EVERYTHING.

WHAT WAS THE RESPONSE?

GATHER UP AS MANY PILLOWS AS POSSIBLE &
TAKE THEM TO A PUBLIC PARK. YELL 'PILLOW
FIGHT!' & LET HUMAN NATURE TAKE OVER.

WHAT WAS THE RESPONSE?

TAKE SOME EXTRA CASH AND TUCK IT INSIDE OF RANDOM DIAPER BOXES AT YOUR LOCAL DISCOUNT STORES.

WHAT WAS THE RESPONSE?

FIGURE 1

AT TOURIST SPOTS, OFFER TO TAKE PHOTOS FOR ANY COUPLES—BUT SNEAK IN A WEIRD ONE OF YOURSELF W/ THE SELFIE CAMERA TOO.

. . . .

. . . .

WHAT WAS THE RESPONSE?

PAY DOUBLE FOR YOUR HAIRCUT & ASK THEM TO GIVE SOMEONE ONE ON THE HOUSE...AND AN EXTRA SPECIAL SCALP MASSAGE.

. . . .

. . . .

WHAT WAS THE RESPONSE?

TAKE A PHOTO OF YOURSELF AND GET IT PRINTED ONTO A FULL SIZE BLANKET. NOW GIVE IT YOUR BEST FRIEND.

. . . .

. . . .

WHAT WAS THE RESPONSE?

RANDOMLY VENMO SOMEONE A TIP FOR ALL
OF THEIR HARD WORK. LIKE THE CREATORS OF
THIS BOOK, JUST FOR AN EXAMPLE.

@BRASSMONKEYGOODS

———————————— WHAT WAS THE RESPONSE? ————————————

DON'T CRUSH THE SPIDERS IN YOUR HOUSE.
CATCH AND RELEASE THEM OUTDOORS SO THEY
CAN LIVE TO TERRORIZE SOME OTHER PERSON.

———————————— WHAT WAS THE RESPONSE? ————————————

GO TO A PARK IN THE FALL AND RAKE ALL OF THE LEAVES INTO ONE GIANT PILE. INVITE EVERYONE WALKING BY TO JUMP IN THEM.

. . . .

. . . .

. . . .

. . . .

. . . .

. . . .

———— WHAT WAS THE RESPONSE? ————

WISH PEOPLE HAPPY BIRTHDAY A DAY EARLY. THEY'LL FEEL SPECIAL BECAUSE YOU CLEARLY REMEMBERED (& NOT A FACEBOOK REMINDER).

PRO-TIP: PUT THEM IN YOUR PHONE FOR A DAY EARLIER THAN THEY ARE

. . . .

. . . .

. . . .

. . . .

. . . .

. . . .

———— WHAT WAS THE RESPONSE? ————

PICK A CO-WORKER THAT YOU RARELY
INTERACT WITH, AND TREAT THEM TO LUNCH.
OR A FREE KITTEN. DEALER'S CHOICE.

WHAT WAS THE RESPONSE?

FIGURE 1

HAND WRITE A REVIEW OF YOUR FAVORITE LOCALLY OWNED COFFEE SHOP, AND TAPE IT ON THEIR FRONT DOOR.

. . . .
. . . .
. . . .
. . . .
. . . .
. . . .
. . . .
. . . .
. . . .
. . . .
. . . .
. . . .
. . . .
. . . .
. . . .
. . . .
. . . .
. . . .
. . . .

RANDOM ACTS OF KINDNESS · NO. 123

WHEN YOU SEE SOMETHING THAT REMINDS YOU OF SOMEONE, TAKE A PICTURE AND TEXT IT TO THEM. UNLESS IT'S, LIKE, DOG POOP.

. . . .

. . . .

——— WHAT WAS THE RESPONSE? ———

RANDOM ACTS OF KINDNESS · NO. 124

FULL SIZE CANDY BARS ARE FOR AMATEURS. NEXT HALLOWEEN, HAND OUT THOSE JUMBO NOVELTY ONES.

. . . .

. . . .

——— WHAT WAS THE RESPONSE? ———

RANDOM ACTS OF KINDNESS · NO. 125

LOOK UP A SECRET CHILDHOOD CRUSH FROM ELEMENTARY SCHOOL—AND SEND THEM A NOTE CONFESSING IT.

. . . .

. . . .

——— WHAT WAS THE RESPONSE? ———

WHEN A FRIEND HAS A SECOND CHILD, BUY THEIR FIRST ONE A GIFT SO THEY KNOW THEY AREN'T FORGOTTEN. LIKE A GIANT DRUM SET.

WHAT WAS THE RESPONSE?

FIGURE 1

PRETEND TO CARE ABOUT CROSSFIT WHILE TALKING TO SOMEONE WHO IS TALKING ABOUT CROSSFIT.

· ·

· ·

· ·

· ·

· ·

· ·

· ·

· ·

· ·

· ·

——————— WHAT WAS THE RESPONSE? ———————

FIGURE 1

CARVE SOME PUMPKINS & LEAVE THEM ON RANDOM DOORSTEPS IN YOUR NEIGHBORHOOD. EXPERT MODE: DO THIS IN JULY.

WHAT WAS THE RESPONSE?

GIVE A FRIEND A DOLLAR'S WORTH OF CRYPTOCURRENCY. IN TEN YEARS THEY COULD BE RICH...OR, LIKELY, HAVE ONE LESS DOLLAR.

WHAT WAS THE RESPONSE?

KEEP PACE BEHIND SOMEONE OUT FOR A JOG WHILE PLAYING THAT ONE 'ROCKY' SONG ON REPEAT THROUGH AN OLD BOOMBOX.

WHAT WAS THE RESPONSE?

GO TO A STORE AND PAY OFF SOME HOLIDAY TOYS ON LAYAWAY—BUT CALL AROUND FIRST. SADLY, FEWER STORES ARE OFFERING IT.

WHAT WAS THE RESPONSE?

PLAY TIC-TAC-TOE WITH THE STRANGER
NEXT TO YOU ON YOUR NEXT FLIGHT.
BEST OUT OF 47 WINS.

NO PAPER? WELL, YOU'RE IN LUCK.

CARE TO MAKE IT INTERESTING? PLACE A BET.

TAKE A FAVORITE BOOK & LEAVE IT ON A BENCH, W/ A NOTE THAT READS '2 THUMBS UP, SAYS A RANDOM PERSON YOU'VE NEVER MET.'

TEXT 'I HAVE NO IDEA WHO YOU ARE,
BUT I HOPE YOU'RE HAVING A WONDERFUL
DAY' TO SOME RANDOM PHONE NUMBERS.

. . . .

. . . .

WHAT WAS THE RESPONSE?

BAKE SOME NESTLÉ TOLL HOUSE COOKIES
& GIVE THEM TO A TOLL BOOTH OPERATOR — BUT
IF THEY DON'T GET IT, TAKE THEM BACK.

. . . .

. . . .

WHAT WAS THE RESPONSE?

THE NEXT TIME YOU GO OUT TO EAT,
ORDER DESSERT — BUT HAVE THE SERVER SEND
IT TO WHATEVER TABLE THEY WANT.

. . . .

. . . .

WHAT WAS THE RESPONSE?

RANDOM ACTS OF KINDNESS · NO. 137

BUY SOME SCRATCH-OFF TICKETS AT THE GAS STATION & HAND THEM OUT TO THE PEOPLE AT EACH PUMP. THEY CAN FIND THEIR OWN COIN.

WHAT WAS THE RESPONSE?

RANDOM ACTS OF KINDNESS · NO. 138

DROP OFF A 12 PACK OF COLD SODA TO A ROAD CONSTRUCTION CREW. ASK THEM IF THEY ENJOY THEIR JOB OF MAKING YOUR LIFE MISERABLE.

WHAT WAS THE RESPONSE?

RANDOM ACTS OF KINDNESS · NO. 139

SURPRISE A VEGETARIAN FRIEND WITH A GIFT. I DON'T KNOW, I GUESS GIVE THEM A BUNCH OF CARROTS OR SOMETHING.

. . . .
. . . .
. . . .
. . . .
. . . .
. . . .
. . . .
. . . .
. . . .
. . . .

──────── WHAT WAS THE RESPONSE? ────────

FIGURE 1

LEARN HOW TO MAKE AN ORIGAMI HEART OUT OF A DOLLAR BILL (*AHEM* GOOGLE IT) AND HAND THEM OUT AS TIPS.

WHAT WAS THE RESPONSE?

FIGURE 1

BUY THE PERSON'S GROCERIES BEHIND YOU IN LINE. IF THEY TRY TO DECLINE, MAKE IT EVEN. PAY & JUST TAKE THEIR MILK OR SOMETHING.

. . . .

. . . .

. . . .

. . . .

. . . .

. . . .

————— WHAT WAS THE RESPONSE? —————

TAKE A DOZEN BAGELS TO YOUR LOCAL POLICE STATION. TELL THEM THAT THEY WERE ALL OUT OF DONUTS.

. . . .

. . . .

. . . .

. . . .

. . . .

. . . .

————— WHAT WAS THE RESPONSE? —————

RANDOM ACTS OF KINDNESS • NO. 143

ORDER A BUNCH OF PIZZAS AND SURPRISE A RETIREMENT HOME WITH DINNER. JUST MAKE SURE IT'S DELIVERED BY 4PM—AT THE LATEST.

WHAT WAS THE RESPONSE?

RANDOM ACTS OF KINDNESS • NO. 144

AFTER A BIG SNOW STORM, MAKE AS MANY SNOWBALLS AS POSSIBLE—THEN START A FIGHT W/ THE NEIGHBORHOOD KIDS. HOLD NO MERCY.

WHAT WAS THE RESPONSE?

RANDOM ACTS OF KINDNESS • NO. 145

GO TO AN AREA ELEMENTARY SCHOOL & ASK TO PAY OFF ANY STUDENT LUNCH DEBT THEY HAVE. ASK FOR SOME CHICKEN NUGGETS TO GO.

WHAT WAS THE RESPONSE?

CARRY AROUND AN AUTOGRAPH BOOK AND
ASK STREET MUSICIANS TO SIGN IT FOR YOU
BECAUSE THEY'LL BE FAMOUS SOMEDAY.

WHAT WAS THE RESPONSE?

DONATE BLOOD. UNLESS IT MAKES YOU
PASS OUT. THEN MAYBE DONATE SOMETHING
THAT DOESN'T COME OUT OF YOUR BODY.

WHAT WAS THE RESPONSE?

TAKE SOME FAST FOOD GIFT CARDS AND PUT
THEM ON THE WINDSHIELDS OF SEMIS PARKED AT
A TRUCK STOP. ALSO: BRING A STEP LADDER.

WHAT WAS THE RESPONSE?

GET SOME BUSINESS CARDS MADE THAT SIMPLY
SAY 'YOU LOOK INCREDIBLE TODAY, BTW.' NOW
HAND THEM TO PEOPLE & JUST WALK AWAY.

WHAT WAS THE RESPONSE?

MAKE YOUR FAVORITE DISH AND DROP IT OFF ON THE PORCH OF A NEIGHBOR'S HOUSE. WRITE DOWN THE RECIPE AND TAPE IT TO THE TOP.

IN A LONG LINE? WRITE THE 1ST WORD OF A
STORY & HAVE THE STRANGER BEHIND YOU WRITE
THE NEXT ONE. TAKE TURNS UNTIL IT'S DONE.

BUY A TINY BOTTLE OF LIQUOR FROM THE
FLIGHT ATTENDANT, BUT ASK THEM NOT TO OPEN
IT. PUT A BOW ON IT & GIVE IT BACK TO THEM.

. . . .

. . . .

. . . .

. . . .

. . . .

. . . .

———————— WHAT WAS THE RESPONSE? ————————

TAKE AN EARLY MORNING WALK ON THE BEACH,
DIG A HOLE IN THE SAND, AND BURY A BAG OF
QUARTERS. MARK THE TOP WITH A BIG X.

. . . .

. . . .

. . . .

. . . .

. . . .

. . . .

———————— WHAT WAS THE RESPONSE? ————————

GIVE AN ICE CREAM TRUCK $100 & HAVE THEM
DRIVE AROUND, GIVING OUT FREE ICE CREAM
UNTIL THE MONEY RUNS OUT. CALL SHOTGUN.

WHAT WAS THE RESPONSE?

IF YOUR GRANDMA IS STILL LIVING,
CALL HER ONCE A WEEK. IF SHE ISN'T, CALL
SOMEONE ELSE'S GRANDMA.

WHAT WAS THE RESPONSE?

MAKE A PAPER AIRPLANE & THROW IT TO A STRANGER ON THE OTHER END OF A SUBWAY CAR. GET THEM TO THROW IT BACK & NOT MUG YOU.

WHAT WAS THE RESPONSE?

PUT TOGETHER A SURPRISE PACKAGE FOR A FRIEND THAT'S MOVED AWAY. INCLUDE ALL OF THEIR LOCAL FAVORITES—LIKE BOOZE.

WHAT WAS THE RESPONSE?

PUT A 'HELP WANTED—12 & UNDER' SIGN IN THE YARD & HIRE ALL THAT APPLY. AFTER MOWING, SEE HOW GOOD BILLY IS AT SPREADSHEETS.

WHAT WAS THE RESPONSE?

LIFT CARRY-ON BAGS INTO THE OVERHEAD BIN
FOR PEOPLE — BUT TELL THEM THAT WE WOULD
BE IN THE AIR ALREADY IF THEY CHECKED THEM.

. . . .

. . . .

. . . .

. . . .

. . . .

. . . .

. . . .

. . . .

. . . .

. . . .

WHAT WAS THE RESPONSE?

FIGURE 1

FIND YOUR OLD ELEMENTARY SCHOOL ART
TEACHER & SEND THEM A SECOND TRY AT AN
OLD PROJECT. ASK FOR EXTRA CREDIT.

DON'T HAVE A CANVAS HANDY? USE THIS:

SIGN YOUR MASTERPIECE

JUST SMILE AT PEOPLE. SERIOUSLY.
THEY MIGHT THINK YOU'RE CRAZY, BUT
WHO CARES.

. . . .

. . . .

. . . .

. . . .

. . . .

. . . .

WHAT WAS THE RESPONSE?

WHENEVER YOU SEE A COIN-OPERATED KIDDIE
RIDE, LEAVE A FEW QUARTERS ON THE
SEAT—AFTER YOU RIDE IT ONCE...FOR TESTING.

. . . .

. . . .

. . . .

. . . .

. . . .

. . . .

WHAT WAS THE RESPONSE?

BEFORE A JOB INTERVIEW, COVER A FRIEND'S CAR IN POST-IT NOTES THAT SAY 'GOOD LUCK!' ALSO, DRIVE THEM TO THE INTERVIEW.

WHAT WAS THE RESPONSE?

FIGURE 1

RANDOM ACTS OF KINDNESS • NO. 164

WHEN YOU'RE IN A BAR THAT HAS A JUKE
BOX, GIVE THE BARTENDER $20 AND LET THEM
PICK. THEY'RE TIRED OF 'PIANO MAN,' TOO.

. . . .
. . . .

——— WHAT WAS THE RESPONSE? ———

RANDOM ACTS OF KINDNESS • NO. 165

HIRE A SKYWRITER TO SPELL OUT SOME
PUNNY INSPIRATIONAL MESSAGE OVER YOUR
TOWN. TRY 'THINGS ARE LOOKING UP.'

.
. . . .
. . . .

——— WHAT WAS THE RESPONSE? ———

RANDOM ACTS OF KINDNESS • NO. 166

WALK AROUND THE PARK IN THE SUMMER,
AND HAND OUT CHEAP KITES TO ANYONE THAT'S
HAVING A PICNIC.

. . . .
. . . .

——— WHAT WAS THE RESPONSE? ———

PICK A RANDOM STREET DOWNTOWN & ADD A QUARTER TO EVERY PARKING METER THAT YOU PASS...MAYBE MORE IF IT'S ABOUT TO EXPIRE.

WHAT WAS THE RESPONSE?

DONATE YOUR OLD FURNITURE TO A LOCAL WOMEN'S SHELTER. IT'S MORE REWARDING THAN SELLING IT TO A CREEPY GUY ON CRAIGSLIST.

WHAT WAS THE RESPONSE?

RANDOM ACTS OF KINDNESS · NO. 169

**IF A STRANGER'S KID STARTS HAVING A
MELTDOWN AT A RESTAURANT, HAVE A DRINK
SENT OVER. FOR THE PARENT, NOT THE CHILD.**

. . . .
. . . .
. . . .
. . . .
. . . .
. . . .

——————— WHAT WAS THE RESPONSE? ———————

RANDOM ACTS OF KINDNESS · NO. 170

**BUY A BUNCH OF RANDOM NAME KEYCHAINS,
& HAND THEM OUT TO THE CASHIERS & SERVERS
THAT YOU COME ACROSS WITH THOSE NAMES.**

. . . .
. . . .
. . . .
. . . .
. . . .
. . . .

——————— WHAT WAS THE RESPONSE? ———————

GET A CARICATURE DONE AT THE FAIR & DRAW
THE ARTIST WHILE THEY'RE DRAWING YOU. IT'LL
BE AWFUL, BUT IT SHOULD MAKE THEM LAUGH.

DON'T HAVE A CANVAS HANDY? USE THIS:

SIGN YOUR MASTERPIECE

STOP TRAFFIC AND HELP AN OLD LADY
CROSS THE STREET. MAKE SURE SHE ACTUALLY
WANTS TO GO OVER THERE FIRST, THOUGH.

WHAT WAS THE RESPONSE?

FIGURE 1

WRITE A POSITIVE REVIEW OF SOME LOCAL GRAFFITI & TAPE IT TO THE WALL. ENCOURAGE THEM TO GO TO ART SCHOOL.

HOLD A GARAGE SALE, AND PUT PRICES ON EVERYTHING—BUT WHEN ANYONE WANTS TO BUY SOMETHING, GIVE IT TO THEM FOR FREE.

. . . .
. . . .

——— WHAT WAS THE RESPONSE? ———

PLAY CHESS WITH A KID & LET THEM WIN. YOU KNOW, SO THEY CAN FEEL BETTER ABOUT THEMSELVES...NOT BECAUSE YOU SUCK AT IT.

. . . .
. . . .

——— WHAT WAS THE RESPONSE? ———

IN THE MIDDLE OF THE NIGHT, SECRETLY WRAP A NEIGHBOR'S TREE IN HOLIDAY LIGHTS AND PLUG IT IN.

. . . .
. . . .

——— WHAT WAS THE RESPONSE? ———

FIND SOME OF THOSE TURN-KNOB CANDY MACHINES AND FILL ALL OF THE SLOTS WITH QUARTERS...BUT DON'T TURN THE KNOBS.

WHAT WAS THE RESPONSE?

FIGURE 1

STUCK IN TRAFFIC? ROLL DOWN YOUR WINDOW AND ASK THE CAR NEXT TO YOU TO PLAY THEIR FAVORITE SONG FOR YOU.

. . . .

. . . .

. . . .

. . . .

. . . .

. . . .

. . . .

. . . .

. . . .

. . . .

——————— WHAT WAS THE RESPONSE? ———————

FIGURE 1

DONATE ALL OF YOUR TOYS TO CHARITY.
NO, NOT THOSE KIND OF TOYS.

WHAT WAS THE RESPONSE?

AFTER THE NEXT SNOW, GO OUT AND SHOVEL
PATHWAYS TO ALL OF YOUR NEIGHBOR'S CARS.
FROM THEIR HOUSES, NOT YOURS.

WHAT WAS THE RESPONSE?

AFTER YOUR NEXT TEETH CLEANING, GIVE
YOUR DENTIST A GOLD STAR AND A CHOICE OF
THREE TOYS FOR BEING SO GOOD.

WHAT WAS THE RESPONSE?

CALL UP YOUR OLD COLLEGE & START A
SCHOLARSHIP IN YOUR NAME. ASK IF $100 AND
A 2 FOR 1 BURRITO COUPON WORKS.

WHAT WAS THE RESPONSE?

DRAW A TATTOO FOR YOUR BEST FRIEND.
NOW MAKE THEM PROMISE THAT THEY'LL GET
IT PUT ON THEIR ARM WHEN YOU DIE.

DON'T HAVE A CANVAS HANDY? USE THIS:

SIGN YOUR MASTERPIECE

IN THE WAITING ROOM, WRITE A POEM OF APPRECIATION FOR THE DOCTOR. EXTRA CREDIT IF YOU CAN RHYME WITH 'HYPOTHALAMUS.'

PUT $10 IN A FEW TINY BOXES, WRAP
THEM UP WITH BOWS, AND LEAVE THEM IN
RANDOM MAIL BOXES.

. . . .
. . . .

WHAT WAS THE RESPONSE?

WHILE ON VACATION, LEAVE A LOVE NOTE FOR
YOUR S.O. IN A STEAMED UP BATHROOM MIRROR.
BONUS, YOU'LL TERRIFY THE NEXT GUEST.

. . . .
. . . .

WHAT WAS THE RESPONSE?

START A WIKIPEDIA PAGE FOR A FAVORITE
BARTENDER — W/ PHOTOS AND A LIST OF THEIR
ACCOMPLISHMENTS. GET OTHERS TO ADD ON.

. . . .
. . . .

WHAT WAS THE RESPONSE?

ASK YOUR THERAPIST HOW THEY'RE DOING. LIKE, DEEP-DOWN INSIDE.

. . . .

. . . .

. . . .

. . . .

. . . .

. . . .

———— WHAT WAS THE RESPONSE? ————

DURING BACK TO SCHOOL SEASON, HANG OUT IN THE SCHOOL SUPPLY AISLE AND RANDOMLY GIVE A FEW PARENTS $10 GIFT CARDS.

. . . .

. . . .

. . . .

. . . .

. . . .

. . . .

———— WHAT WAS THE RESPONSE? ————

TEXT A RANDOM CONTACT IN YOUR PHONE EACH DAY FOR A WEEK. JUST SAY HI. FOLLOWED BY NO, YOU HAVEN'T BEEN DRINKING.

. . . .
. . . .
. . . .
. . . .
. . . .
. . . .
. . . .
. . . .
. . . .
. . . .

———— WHAT WAS THE RESPONSE? ————

FIGURE 1

TRY TO HOLD AN ELEVATOR FOR SOMEONE – BUT
LIKELY GET CONFUSED ABOUT WHICH BUTTON TO
PUSH AND ACCIDENTALLY CLOSE IT ON THEM.

. . . .
. . . .
. . . .
. . . .
. . . .
. . . .
. . . .
. . . .
. . . .
. . . .
. . . .

———————— WHAT WAS THE RESPONSE? ————————

FIGURE 1

DROP OFF S'MORE MAKING SUPPLIES TO THE LOCAL FIRE DEPARTMENT.

WHAT WAS THE RESPONSE?

GIVE SOMEONE A COMPLIMENT IN THE GYM LOCKER ROOM...BUT MAYBE WAIT UNTIL THEY'RE NOT NAKED.

WHAT WAS THE RESPONSE?

ONE WEEK, TRY TO BUY ALL YOUR GROCERIES AT THE FARMER'S MARKET. YOU'LL PROBABLY HAVE TO ASK AROUND FOR THE PIZZA ROLLS.

WHAT WAS THE RESPONSE?

BUY 20 HAPPY MEALS AT MCDONALD'S & HAND THEM OUT TO THE CARS WAITING IN THE DRIVE THRU...REGARDLESS OF IF THEY HAVE KIDS.

WHAT WAS THE RESPONSE?

BUY YOUR FRIEND'S DOG A CHRISTMAS GIFT. IF THEIR DOG IS JEWISH, BUY THEM 8 GIFTS.

. . . .
. . . .
. . . .
. . . .
. . . .
. . . .
. . . .
. . . .
. . . .
. . . .

—————— WHAT WAS THE RESPONSE? ——————

FIGURE 1

RENT OUT A BILLBOARD TO THANK YOUR MOM & DAD FOR EVERYTHING THEY TAUGHT YOU...EXCEPT FOR FISCAL RESPONSIBILITY.

WHAT WAS THE RESPONSE?

FIGURE 1

ON YOUR NEXT TRIP, BUY SOUVENIRS FOR YOUR
FRIENDS — SO THEY KNOW YOU WERE THINKING
OF THEM WHILE HAVING FUN WITHOUT THEM.

. . . .
. . . .
. . . .
. . . .
. . . .
. . . .

——————— WHAT WAS THE RESPONSE? ———————

GO SEE A FRIEND'S IMPROV SHOW.
ALSO, PRAY TO GOD THAT THEY ARE
SOMEWHAT DECENT AT IMPROV.

. . . .
. . . .
. . . .
. . . .
. . . .
. . . .

——————— WHAT WAS THE RESPONSE? ———————

RANDOM ACTS OF KINDNESS • NO. 200

**GO TO A LIBRARY AND ASK TO PAY OFF
SOMEONE'S FINES. MAYBE THEY'LL TURN OVER
A NEW LEAF AND STOP BEING SUCH A MENACE.**

. . . .
. . . .

——— WHAT WAS THE RESPONSE? ———

RANDOM ACTS OF KINDNESS • NO. 201

USE CHALK TO WRITE INSPIRATIONAL MESSAGES
ON THE SIDEWALK. LIKE 'YOU'VE GOT THIS' IN
FRONT OF A PORT-A-POTTY.

. . . .
. . . .

——— WHAT WAS THE RESPONSE? ———

RANDOM ACTS OF KINDNESS • NO. 202

**DONATE TO A LGBTQ+ CHARITY IN
THE NAME OF SOME HOMOPHOBE THAT
YOU DON'T LIKE.**

. . . .
. . . .

——— WHAT WAS THE RESPONSE? ———

TELL SOMEONE WHEN THEY LOOK LIKE A
CELEBRITY. JUST DON'T SPECIFY WHICH ONE.
ESPECIALLY IF IT'S STEVE BUSCEMI.

WHAT WAS THE RESPONSE?

INSPIRE OTHERS TO BE KIND BY
WRITING A BOOK FULL OF RANDOM ACTS OF
KINDNESS...OR JUST BUY THEM THIS ONE.

WHAT WAS THE RESPONSE?

RANDOM ACTS OF KINDNESS • NO. 205

AFTER A SNOWSTORM, DROP OFF SOME SLEDS
AT A LOCAL HILL BEFORE DAWN...BUT GO AHEAD
AND TRY THEM OUT WHILE YOU'RE THERE.

WHAT WAS THE RESPONSE?

RANDOM ACTS OF KINDNESS • NO. 206

ORDER FOOD ON A DELIVERY SERVICE LIKE
GRUBHUB. IN THE SPECIAL NOTES, WRITE 'MARK
IT COMPLETE & KEEP THE FOOD, IT'S ON ME.'

WHAT WAS THE RESPONSE?

DRAW A COUPON FOR A FREE FOOT MASSAGE &
LEAVE IT ON A PARK BENCH. BOOM—SOMEONE'S
GETTIN' A FOOT RUB WHEN THEY GET HOME.

DON'T HAVE A CANVAS HANDY? USE THIS:

SIGN YOUR MASTERPIECE

PUT A SANDWICH IN THE WORK FRIDGE W/ AN
AGGRESSIVELY-POSITIVE NOTE, LIKE 'SOMEONE
BETTER EAT THIS FREE FOOD OR I MIGHT SNAP.'

FILL A 10 GALLON ZIPLOC BAG W/ MICROWAVE POPCORN AND GO TO A DRIVE-IN MOVIE—NOW GO CAR TO CAR GIVING IT ALL AWAY.

. . . .

. . . .

. . . .

. . . .

. . . .

. . . .

. . . .

——————— WHAT WAS THE RESPONSE? ———————

TEACH SOMEONE HOW TO DRIVE A STICK SHIFT...BUT USE THEIR CAR—UNLESS YOU WANT TO GIFT YOURSELF A NEW CLUTCH.

. . . .

. . . .

. . . .

. . . .

. . . .

. . . .

. . . .

——————— WHAT WAS THE RESPONSE? ———————

TREAT EVERYBODY ON YOUR NEXT ROLLER COASTER RIDE TO THE OVERPRICED PHOTO OF THEMSELVES SCREAMING.

. . . .
. . . .
. . . .
. . . .
. . . .
. . . .

——————— WHAT WAS THE RESPONSE? ———————

BUILD A GIANT SLIP & SLIDE IN YOUR FRONT YARD AND INVITE THE NEIGHBORHOOD OVER. PRO-TIP: CHECK FOR ANY ROCKS FIRST.

. . . .
. . . .
. . . .
. . . .
. . . .
. . . .

——————— WHAT WAS THE RESPONSE? ———————

SHARE YOUR FAVORITE HIDDEN GEM
RESTAURANT WITH OTHERS, NO MATTER HOW
MUCH YOU WANT TO KEEP IT TO YOURSELF.

@SHOPSINSNYC — YOU'RE WELCOME. TELL ZACK & LUKE WE SAID HI.

· ·

· ·

———— WHAT WAS THE RESPONSE? ————

RENT A LIMO FOR YOUR FRIEND TO RUN
ERRANDS W/ FOR A DAY. FIRST STOP, ALDI. ASK
IF THE DRIVER HAS A QUARTER FOR A CART.

· ·

· ·

———— WHAT WAS THE RESPONSE? ————

ASK SOMEONE IF THEY KNOW WHAT TIME IT IS.
IF THEY ANSWER, JUST SAY 'THAT'S CORRECT.
CONGRATULATIONS!' AND GIVE THEM $5.

· ·

· ·

———— WHAT WAS THE RESPONSE? ————

TAKE YOUR OLD TROPHIES & GET NEW
PLAQUES MADE FOR THEM THAT SAY 'BEST
PERSON EVER.' NOW GIVE THEM OUT.

WHAT WAS THE RESPONSE?

FIGURE 1

MAKE A LIST OF POSSIBLE VANITY LICENSE PLATE IDEAS FOR YOUR FRIENDS & FAMILY—AND SHARE THE ONES THAT AREN'T INSULTING.

RANDOM ACTS OF KINDNESS • NO. 218

HEAD TO THE PENNY SLOT AREA OF
A CASINO AND GIVE EACH PERSON PLAYING
A ROLL OF...WELL...PENNIES.

WHAT WAS THE RESPONSE?

RANDOM ACTS OF KINDNESS • NO. 219

GO TO ITALY AND GIVE EVERYONE
TRYING TO HOLD UP THE LEANING TOWER
OF PISA HIGH-FIVES.

WHAT WAS THE RESPONSE?

OFFER TO MURDER, I MEAN WATER, SOMEONE'S PLANTS FOR THEM WHEN THEY GO ON VACATION.

WHAT WAS THE RESPONSE?

FIGURE 1

RANDOM ACTS OF KINDNESS • NO. 221

DELETE YOUR SOCIAL MEDIA & SPEND MORE TIME TALKING TO THE PEOPLE YOU CARE ABOUT. OR FOLLOW US @BRASSMONKEYGOODS.

· ·
· ·

——— WHAT WAS THE RESPONSE? ———

RANDOM ACTS OF KINDNESS • NO. 222

ORGANIZE AN OUTDOOR MOVIE NIGHT ON YOUR STREET–OR JUST START PROJECTING THEM ON YOUR NEIGHBOR'S HOUSE & SEE WHAT HAPPENS.

· ·
· ·

——— WHAT WAS THE RESPONSE? ———

RANDOM ACTS OF KINDNESS • NO. 223

PASS SOMEONE STRUGGLING WITH A FLAT TIRE? CALL ROADSIDE ASSISTANCE AND PAY TO HAVE SOMEONE CHANGE IT FOR THEM.

STOPPING ON THE SIDE OF THE ROAD IS DANGEROUS. HAVE AN EXPERT HELP.

· ·
· ·

——— WHAT WAS THE RESPONSE? ———

OFFER A STRANGER A SHOULDER
TO CRY ON. IN FACT, LET THEM GET YOUR
SHOULDER AS WET AS THEY NEED TO.

WHAT WAS THE RESPONSE?

MENTOR STUDENTS THAT ARE STUDYING
TO GO INTO YOUR LINE OF WORK. IN FACT, IF
YOU'RE A DESIGN STUDENT, EMAIL US.

MIKE@BRASSMONKEYGOODS.COM · MELANIE@BRASSMONKEYGOODS.COM

WHAT WAS THE RESPONSE?

HOUSE SIT FOR FRIENDS & FAMILY. I MEAN THEY ALREADY KNOW HOW GREAT YOU ARE AT SITTING.

WHAT WAS THE RESPONSE?

IF YOU'RE AT A BAR WHEN IT'S CLOSING, ORDER A RIDE FOR ANY PATRONS THAT MIGHT NEED ONE – YOURSELF INCLUDED.

WHAT WAS THE RESPONSE?

RANDOM ACTS OF KINDNESS · NO. 228

ASK A CO-WORKER TO DRAW THEIR DREAM CAR. THE NEXT DAY, SURPRISE THEM WITH IT—THEIR DRAWING, FRAMED.

DON'T HAVE A CANVAS HANDY? USE THIS:

SIGN YOUR MASTERPIECE

LIST ALL OF THE CHARITIES & ORGANIZATIONS
THAT ARE MEANINGFUL TO YOU. NOW TRY TO
DONATE TO EACH ONE—NO MATTER HOW SMALL.

GO TO THE LOCAL ANIMAL SHELTER & ADOPT
ONE. IF FOR SOME REASON YOU CAN'T, PRE-PAY
FOR THE NEXT PERSON THAT COMES IN.

. . . .
. . . .
. . . .
. . . .
. . . .
. . . .
. . . .
. . . .
. . . .
. . . .

——————— WHAT WAS THE RESPONSE? ———————

FIGURE 1

RENT A FOOD TRUCK FOR THE AFTERNOON, PARK IT OUTSIDE OF A LOCAL HOSPITAL, AND LET ALL OF THE WORKERS EAT FOR FREE.

. . . .
. . . .

———— WHAT WAS THE RESPONSE? ————

GO CHEER ON A LOCAL HIGH SCHOOL SPORTS TEAM, EVEN IF YOU DON'T HAVE ANY KIDS THAT GO THERE...OR UNDERSTAND SPORTS.

. . . .
. . . .

———— WHAT WAS THE RESPONSE? ————

ACTUALLY TELL YOUR MOM HOW AMAZING HER COOKING IS...OR, DEPENDING ON YOUR MOM, HOW GREAT SHE IS AT REHEATING TAKE-OUT.

. . . .
. . . .

———— WHAT WAS THE RESPONSE? ————

BUY A COUPLE HUNDRED TENNIS BALLS
AND PILE THEM IN THE MIDDLE OF YOUR
LOCAL DOG PARK.

WHAT WAS THE RESPONSE?

FIGURE 1

IF SOMEONE'S CAR WINDOW WAS LEFT DOWN IN A RAIN STORM, COVER IT W/ SOMETHING. USE YOUR SHIRT FOR THE SEXIEST SOLUTION.

. . . .

. . . .

. . . .

. . . .

. . . .

. . . .

. . . .

. . . .

. . . .

. . . .

WHAT WAS THE RESPONSE?

FIGURE 1

ASK YOUR BARISTA HOW THEIR WEEKEND WAS,
EVEN IF ALL YOU REALLY WANT IS YOUR BLOODY
COFFEE ALREADY AND IT'S A THURSDAY.

WHAT WAS THE RESPONSE?

ORGANIZE YOUR BEST FRIENDS BACHELOR
AND/OR BACHELORETTE PARTY. EITHER WAY,
RENT A BOUNCE HOUSE.

WHAT WAS THE RESPONSE?

PUT TOGETHER CARE PACKAGES OF WARM
SOCKS AND TOILETRIES, AND HAND THEM OUT
TO THE HOMELESS.

WHAT WAS THE RESPONSE?

GIVE AWAY YOUR SEAT WHILE WAITING AT
A CROWDED GATE BEFORE A FLIGHT—BUT ONCE
IT BOARDS, IT'S EVERY MAN FOR HIMSELF.

WHAT WAS THE RESPONSE?

LEAVE SOMEONE A NOTE COMPLIMENTING
THEIR MOTORCYCLE...SOMETHING TO THE EFFECT
OF 'THIS DEATHTRAP SURE IS GORGEOUS.'

DRAW AN ELABORATE SANDCASTLE, AND
HIRE KIDS AT THE BEACH TO BUILD IT FOR YOU.
PAY THEM IN ICE CREAM.

DON'T HAVE A CANVAS HANDY? USE THIS:

SIGN YOUR MASTERPIECE

TELL EVERY PERSON AT WORK WHAT YOU THINK THEY ARE GREAT AT. LIKE ANNOYING THE CRAP OUT OF YOU, FOR A REALLY BAD EXAMPLE.

WHAT WAS THE RESPONSE?

GIVE THE CASHIER AT GOODWILL $100 AND TELL THEM TO PAY FOR EVERYTHING THEY RING UP UNTIL IT RUNS OUT.

WHAT WAS THE RESPONSE?

DO SOMETHING NICE FOR A CAT: LEAVE IT ALONE, FEED IT, AND OTHERWISE TRY NOT TO ACKNOWLEDGE IT.

WHAT WAS THE RESPONSE?

ON A 90 DEGREE DAY, FILL A 50 GALLON TRASH CAN W/ WATER BALLOONS AND TELL THE NEIGHBORHOOD KIDS TO THROW THEM AT YOU.

—————— WHAT WAS THE RESPONSE? ——————

GIVE A SUBTLE THUMBS UP TO STRANGERS WHEN THEY COME OUT OF A FITTING ROOM TO SEE HOW SOMETHING FITS.

—————— WHAT WAS THE RESPONSE? ——————

PRETEND TO LIKE THE SONG THAT YOUR FRIEND WITH HORRIBLE TASTE IN MUSIC JUST SHARED WITH YOU.

WHAT WAS THE RESPONSE?

FIGURE 1

LEAVE A BOX OF DIAPERS IN THE FAMILY RESTROOM. IF IT'S A CRACKER BARREL, LEAVE A BOX OF ADULT DIAPERS TOO.

. . . .

. . . .

. . . .

. . . .

. . . .

. . . .

. . . .

. . . .

. . . .

. . . .

——————— WHAT WAS THE RESPONSE? ———————

FIGURE 1

PUT POST-ITS ON THE MIRRORS IN YOUR GYM THAT SAY 'WOW, HAVE YOU BEEN WORKING OUT?'

WHAT WAS THE RESPONSE?

ACTUALLY LISTEN TO YOUR DAD'S VOICEMAIL, EVEN THOUGH YOU ALREADY KNOW IT SAYS 'HEY, CALL ME BACK.'

WHAT WAS THE RESPONSE?

AFTER YOU MOVE, GIVE YOUR EMPTY MOVING
BOXES AWAY ON CRAIGSLIST. WHEN THEY PICK
THEM UP, THROW IN A CASE OF COLD BEER.*

*UNLESS THEY ARE UNDERAGE OF COURSE. IN THAT CASE: JUICE BOXES.

WHAT WAS THE RESPONSE?

COMMISSION AN ARTIST TO PAINT YOUR BEST
FRIEND'S DOG—ON A CANVAS TO BE SPECIFIC.
THAT WOULD NEVER WASH OUT OF THEIR FUR.

WHAT WAS THE RESPONSE?

DRAW A HANDMADE VALENTINE'S CARD FOR YOUR PARTNER. VOILÁ—YOU JUST SAVED $10 TO SPEND ON MEDIOCRE WINE.

DON'T HAVE A CANVAS HANDY? USE THIS:

SIGN YOUR MASTERPIECE

MAKE A LIST OF ALL OF THE PEOPLE YOU ARE
THANKFUL FOR, AND INVITE THEM ALL OVER
FOR THANKSGIVING. OH, AND GOOD LUCK.

STAND AT THE END OF A TALL SLIDE AT A WATER PARK & TELL THE PEOPLE GETTING OFF IF ANY 'BODY PARTS' POPPED OUT OF THEIR SWIMSUIT.

. . . .

. . . .

. . . .

. . . .

. . . .

. . . .

———— WHAT WAS THE RESPONSE? ————

OHH AND AHH OVER YOUR CO-WORKERS NEW BABY, EVEN IF IT HAPPENS TO LOOK LIKE A SNOTTY LITTLE ALIEN.

. . . .

. . . .

. . . .

. . . .

. . . .

. . . .

———— WHAT WAS THE RESPONSE? ————

VOLUNTEER TO MAKE BALLOON ANIMALS AT A KID'S BIRTHDAY PARTY—HOPEFULLY THEY LIKE SNAKES.

WHAT WAS THE RESPONSE?

SURPRISE A FRIEND ON THEIR BIRTHDAY. TELL THEM TO CLOSE THEIR EYES & DRIVE THEM TO AN AMAZING RESTAURANT...IN ANOTHER STATE.

WHAT WAS THE RESPONSE?

RANDOM ACTS OF KINDNESS • NO. 259

STOP AT DUMB ROADSIDE ATTRACTIONS & BUY A SOUVENIR FOR ANYONE ELSE THERE—HELP KEEP THE WORLD'S LARGEST BALL OF TWINE ALIVE.

. . . .
. . . .

WHAT WAS THE RESPONSE?

RANDOM ACTS OF KINDNESS • NO. 260

PERSONALLY COMPLIMENT THE SINGERS AT A KARAOKE BAR AFTER THEIR PERFORMANCES—NOW GO BACK TO YOUR TABLE & BEG TO LEAVE.

. . . .
. . . .

WHAT WAS THE RESPONSE?

RANDOM ACTS OF KINDNESS • NO. 261

LEAVE A CANDY BAR (AND A TIP) FOR THE PERSON CLEANING YOUR HOTEL ROOM. JUST NOT FROM THE MINIBAR...THOSE ARE LIKE $12!

. . . .
. . . .

WHAT WAS THE RESPONSE?

WHEN YOU BUY A NEW PIECE OF CLOTHING,
DONATE SOMETHING YOU DON'T WEAR TO THE
RED CROSS—LIKE THAT ED HARDY SHIRT.

WHAT WAS THE RESPONSE?

FIGURE 1

**DRAW A BOUQUET OF FLOWERS & HAND IT
TO SOMEONE AT THE BUS STOP. THEY'LL EITHER
LOVE IT, OR THINK YOU GAVE THEM GARBAGE.**

DON'T HAVE A CANVAS HANDY? USE THIS:

SIGN YOUR MASTERPIECE

WHEN SOMEONE HAS A REALLY DUMB IDEA IN
A MEETING, NOD ALONG LIKE YOU UNDERSTAND
WHAT THE HELL THEY'RE GOING ON ABOUT.

WHAT WAS THE RESPONSE?

WALK AROUND THE CLUBHOUSE OF A GOLF
COURSE AND OFFER TO WASH PEOPLE'S BALLS
FOR THEM—UNTIL THEY KICK YOU OUT.

WHAT WAS THE RESPONSE?

ON YOUR NEXT TRIP, BRING A GIFT FOR THE
TSA AGENT. JUST MAKE SURE IT'S UNDER 3.4 OZ
AND IN A CLEAR ZIPLOC BAG—WITH A BOW.

WHAT WAS THE RESPONSE?

FIGURE 1

RANDOM ACTS OF KINDNESS • NO. 267

THE NEXT TIME YOU SEE A COTTON CANDY
VENDOR, BUY SOME. HELP PRESERVE THE ART
OF SELLING PEOPLE SUGAR-COATED AIR.

. . . .
. . . .

——— WHAT WAS THE RESPONSE? ———

RANDOM ACTS OF KINDNESS • NO. 268

START A BOOK CLUB FOR YOUR FRIENDS.
ALSO INFORM YOUR FRIENDS THAT BY 'BOOK'
YOU MEAN 'DAY DRINKING' ON A SCHEDULE.

. . . .
. . . .

——— WHAT WAS THE RESPONSE? ———

RANDOM ACTS OF KINDNESS • NO. 269

NEXT TIME YOU'RE IN STAND-STILL TRAFFIC,
OFFER THE CAR NEXT TO YOU A SNACK.
PREREQUISITE: KEEP SNACKS IN YOUR CAR.

. . . .
. . . .

——— WHAT WAS THE RESPONSE? ———

DRIVE SOMEONE TO CHURCH, BUT INSIST ON PLAYING THAT HOZIER SONG ON REPEAT UNTIL YOU GET THERE.

....

....

....

....

....

....

——————— WHAT WAS THE RESPONSE? ———————

ASK ABOUT, AND ENCOURAGE, OTHER PEOPLE'S HOBBIES, NO MATTER HOW BIG OF A WASTE OF TIME THEY MIGHT BE.

....

....

....

....

....

....

——————— WHAT WAS THE RESPONSE? ———————

DRESS YOUR PETS UP IN CUTE CLOTHES. THE KINDNESS PART IS WHEN YOU FINALLY TAKE IT OFF OF THEM.

— WHAT WAS THE RESPONSE? —

STOP AT A HIGHWAY GAS STATION ON YOUR NEXT ROAD TRIP, AND BUY A ROLLER HOT DOG FOR THE FIRST TEN PEOPLE THAT COME IN.

— WHAT WAS THE RESPONSE? —

DRAW PORTRAITS OF YOURSELF MEETING
YOUR PARTNER—BEFORE & AFTER. PRO-TIP: YOU
SHOULD BE SMILING IN THE AFTER ONE.

DON'T HAVE A CANVAS HANDY? USE THIS:

SIGN YOUR MASTERPIECE

BUY A LOTTERY TICKET & GIVE IT BACK TO THE
CASHIER—BUT ADD YOUR PHONE NUMBER, JUST
IN CASE IT WINS & THEY WANT TO BE KIND TOO.

WHAT WAS THE RESPONSE?

FIGURE 1

MAKE A LIST OF EVERYONE THAT YOU WOULD LOVE TO PUNCH IN THE FACE. NOW TRY REALLY HARD NOT TO.

. . . .

. . . .

. . . .

. . . .

. . . .

. . . .

. . . .

. . . .

. . . .

. . . .

. . . .

. . . .

. . . .

. . . .

. . . .

. . . .

. . . .

. . . .

. . . .

. . . .

MAKE SOCK PUPPETS OF ALL OF YOUR
FRIENDS FOR GIFTS. NOW FORCE THEM TO
PUT ON A PUPPET SHOW FOR YOU.

— WHAT WAS THE RESPONSE? —

PLANT SOME BEE-FRIENDLY FLOWERS. IT
DOESN'T HAVE TO BE IN YOUR YARD—SURPRISE
YOUR NEIGHBORS.

— WHAT WAS THE RESPONSE? —

GIVE A SLEEVE OF MENTOS TO YOUR
MENTOR AND WHISPER 'THE FRESHMAKER.'
IF THEY DON'T LAUGH, GET A NEW MENTOR.

— WHAT WAS THE RESPONSE? —

PAY FOR A FRIEND TO DO AN ESCAPE ROOM.
ALSO, PAY THE ATTENDANT TO MAKE SURE THAT
IT'S NOT SOLVABLE.

. . . .
. . . .
. . . .
. . . .
. . . .
. . . .
. . . .
. . . .
. . . .
. . . .
. . . .

——————— WHAT WAS THE RESPONSE? ———————

FIGURE 1

CARRY AROUND A ZIPPO IN CASE A SMOKER FRIEND NEEDS A LIGHT. BE SURE TO TELL THEM HOW MUCH YOU'LL MISS THEM WHEN THEY DIE.

. . . .

. . . .

. . . .

. . . .

. . . .

. . . .

. . . .

. . . .

. . . .

. . . .

———— WHAT WAS THE RESPONSE? ————

FIGURE 1

WAVE AND SMILE AT LITERALLY EVERYONE
YOU SEE FOR AN ENTIRE DAY. TRY TO AVOID
BEING COMMITTED.

WHAT WAS THE RESPONSE?

HAVE A CASE OF DEODORANT GIFT-WRAPPED
& SENT TO THE COACH OF A MIDDLE SCHOOL
FOOTBALL TEAM.

WHAT WAS THE RESPONSE?

GET YOUR FRIEND THAT LOVES CYCLING A
TANDEM BICYCLE SO YOU CAN DO IT TOGETHER.
DON'T BOTHER PEDALING, THEY ENJOY IT.

WHAT WAS THE RESPONSE?

ACTUALLY UNJAM THE PRINTER AT WORK,
INSTEAD OF JUST LEAVING IT LIKE SOME
KIND OF MONSTER.

WHAT WAS THE RESPONSE?

HIDE TWENTY BUCKS SOMEWHERE AROUND
TOWN—NOW DRAW A TREASURE MAP AND TAPE
IT TO A SWING AT THE PLAYGROUND.

DON'T HAVE A CANVAS HANDY? USE THIS:

SIGN YOUR MASTERPIECE

KEEP A LIST OF FRIENDS' FAVORITE FOODS TO RANDOMLY SURPRISE THEM WITH—OR TO EAT IN FRONT OF THEM IF THEY MAKE YOU MAD.

. . . .

. . . .

. . . .

. . . .

. . . .

. . . .

. . . .

. . . .

. . . .

. . . .

. . . .

. . . .

. . . .

. . . .

. . . .

. . . .

. . . .

. . . .

. . . .

. . . .

———— NO PAPER? WELL, YOU'RE IN LUCK. ————

SELLING YOUR CAR? TUCK A GREETING CARD INSIDE CONGRATULATING THE NEXT OWNER—AND THROW IN $20 FOR GAS.

WHAT WAS THE RESPONSE?

GATHER UP ALL THE BOOKS IN YOUR HOUSE THAT YOU'LL PROBABLY NEVER ACTUALLY READ AND DONATE THEM TO A PRISON LIBRARY.

WHAT WAS THE RESPONSE?

BUY AS MANY GIRL SCOUT COOKIES AS POSSIBLE TO, YOU KNOW, SUPPORT THE GIRL SCOUTS AND FOR NO OTHER REASON.

WHAT WAS THE RESPONSE?

**PROACTIVELY TELL THE TICKET AGENT TO HAVE
A NICE FLIGHT THE NEXT TIME THEY TAKE A
TRIP—JUST SO IT'S CLEAR IT WAS ON PURPOSE.**

. . . .

. . . .

. . . .

. . . .

. . . .

. . . .

———————— WHAT WAS THE RESPONSE? ————————

**IF YOU HAVE ANY MONEY LEFT AFTER
DOING ALL OF THOSE, MAYBE BUY YOURSELF
A DRINK & TAKE A NAP. YOU DESERVE IT.**

. . . .

. . . .

. . . .

. . . .

. . . .

. . . .

———————— WHAT WAS THE RESPONSE? ————————

WRITE DOWN SOME THINGS THAT STRANGERS HAVE DONE FOR YOU, AND DO THEM FOR OTHERS. GETTING FLIPPED OFF DOESN'T COUNT.

DON'T STOP WITH ONE. USE THE NEXT FEW PAGES TOO.

RANDOM ACTS OF KINDNESS · PAY IT FORWARD

WHAT WAS THE RESPONSE?

RANDOM ACTS OF KINDNESS · PAY IT FORWARD

WHAT WAS THE RESPONSE?

RANDOM ACTS OF KINDNESS • PAY IT FORWARD

WHAT WAS THE RESPONSE?

RANDOM ACTS OF KINDNESS • PAY IT FORWARD

WHAT WAS THE RESPONSE?

RANDOM ACTS OF KINDNESS • PAY IT FORWARD

WHAT WAS THE RESPONSE?

RANDOM ACTS OF KINDNESS • PAY IT FORWARD

WHAT WAS THE RESPONSE?

WHAT WAS THE RESPONSE?

RANDOM ACTS OF KINDNESS • PAY IT FORWARD

WHAT WAS THE RESPONSE?

RANDOM ACTS OF KINDNESS • PAY IT FORWARD

_____

_____

· ·

· ·

· ·

· ·

· ·

· ·

————————— WHAT WAS THE RESPONSE? —————————

RANDOM ACTS OF KINDNESS • PAY IT FORWARD

_____

_____

· ·

· ·

· ·

· ·

· ·

· ·

————————— WHAT WAS THE RESPONSE? —————————

RANDOM ACTS OF KINDNESS • PAY IT FORWARD

. . . .
. . . .
. . . .
. . . .
. . . .
. . . .

———— **WHAT WAS THE RESPONSE?** ————

RANDOM ACTS OF KINDNESS • PAY IT FORWARD

. . . .
. . . .
. . . .
. . . .
. . . .
. . . .

———— **WHAT WAS THE RESPONSE?** ————

RANDOM ACTS OF KINDNESS • PAY IT FORWARD

WHAT WAS THE RESPONSE?

RANDOM ACTS OF KINDNESS • PAY IT FORWARD

WHAT WAS THE RESPONSE?

THINK YOU CAN DO BETTER? LET'S SEE IT. NOW IT'S YOUR TURN TO COME UP WITH YOUR OWN ACTS OF KINDNESS...AND DO THEM.

PSST: SHARE THEM WITH US @BRASSMONKEYGOODS

NO PAPER? WELL, YOU'RE IN LUCK.

RANDOM ACTS OF KINDNESS • NOW IT'S YOUR TURN

WHAT WAS THE RESPONSE?

RANDOM ACTS OF KINDNESS • NOW IT'S YOUR TURN

WHAT WAS THE RESPONSE?

RANDOM ACTS OF KINDNESS · NOW IT'S YOUR TURN

WHAT WAS THE RESPONSE?

RANDOM ACTS OF KINDNESS · NOW IT'S YOUR TURN

WHAT WAS THE RESPONSE?

RANDOM ACTS OF KINDNESS • NOW IT'S YOUR TURN

WHAT WAS THE RESPONSE?

RANDOM ACTS OF KINDNESS • NOW IT'S YOUR TURN

WHAT WAS THE RESPONSE?

RANDOM ACTS OF KINDNESS • NOW IT'S YOUR TURN

WHAT WAS THE RESPONSE?

RANDOM ACTS OF KINDNESS • NOW IT'S YOUR TURN

WHAT WAS THE RESPONSE?

RANDOM ACTS OF KINDNESS • NOW IT'S YOUR TURN

WHAT WAS THE RESPONSE?

RANDOM ACTS OF KINDNESS • NOW IT'S YOUR TURN

WHAT WAS THE RESPONSE?

RANDOM ACTS OF KINDNESS • NOW IT'S YOUR TURN

. . . .
. . . .
. . . .
. . . .
. . . .
. . . .

WHAT WAS THE RESPONSE?

RANDOM ACTS OF KINDNESS • NOW IT'S YOUR TURN

. . . .
. . . .
. . . .
. . . .
. . . .
. . . .

WHAT WAS THE RESPONSE?

BRASSMONKEYGOODS.COM

✖

@BRASSMONKEYGOODS 📷